Pompeii

UNEARTHING ANCIENT WORLDS

Liz Sonneborn

Twenty-First Century Books • Minneapolis

Twenty-First Century Books
A division of Lerner Publishing Group, Inc.
241 First Avenue North
Minneapolis, MN 55401 U.S.A.

Website address: www.lernerbooks.com

Library of Congress Cataloging-in-Publication Data

Sonneborn, Liz.
    Pompeii / by Liz Sonneborn.
        p.   cm. — (Unearthing ancient worlds)
    Includes bibliographical references and index.
    ISBN-13: 978–0–8225–7505–4 (lib. bdg. : alk. paper)
        1. Excavations (Archaeology)—Italy—Pompeii (Extinct city)—History—Juvenile literature.
    2. Excavations (Archaeology)—Italy—Herculaneum (Extinct city)—History—Juvenile literature.
    3. Vesuvius Region—Antiquities, Roman—Juvenile literature. I. Title.
    DG70.P7S735 2008
    937'.7—dc22   2007022058

Manufactured in the United States of America
1 2 3 4 5 6 – PA – 13 12 11 10 09 08

TABLE OF CONTENTS

An eighteenth-century French artist painted this imagined scene of Mount Vesuvius erupting in A.D. 79 and burying the city of Pompeii. The Roman historian, Pliny the Elder, is on the beach about to be covered with lava.

INTRODUCTION

The day—August 24, A.D. 79—began much like any other in Pompeii. Pompeii was a port city of the ancient Roman Empire. Shopkeepers laid out their wares and tended to their customers. Craftspeople gathered at workshops and began their daily work. People filled the streets, busily attending to their chores.

But many people in Pompeii were feeling a little uneasy. In the last few days, the city had been disturbed by a series of small earthquakes. Just seventeen years earlier, much of the city was destroyed by the massive quake of A.D. 62. Some residents had moved away. But most people had stayed. They set about repairing their homes and other buildings. The reconstruction was still going strong, when suddenly Pompeii faced a far greater and far deadlier natural disaster.

Pompeii lay in the shadow of the great Mount Vesuvius. Vesuvius, a volcano, hadn't erupted in hundreds of years. The people who lived in the towns at its foot didn't know that they had anything to fear. But that afternoon, August 24, at about one o'clock, an enormous mass of ash, gas, and rocks spewed out of Vesuvius's cone. The volcanic matter shot up into the air. It rose nearly 100,000 feet (30,000 meters) high before spreading out across the sky.

The wind carried away small clumps of volcanic material called lapilli. By about 3 o'clock, these lapilli began to rain down onto Pompeii

In the 1800s, archaeologists learned to make plaster casts of the decayed bodies that had been buried in the lava at Pompeii centuries before.

and surrounding towns. People ran through the streets. Desperately, they looked for places to hide. Each tiny lapillus alone was too small to hurt anyone. But as more and more fell, they began to build up. Under the weight of inches of lapilli, roofs of buildings caved in. They trapped and killed those seeking shelter inside.

People scurried around. They gathered their valuables and hoped to escape from the city. But dense clouds of volcanic dust filled the air. The clouds made it difficult to find a way out. Finally, at dawn, the air began to clear. Pompeii's residents started to breathe a sigh of relief. But at that moment, lava—melted, liquid rock—began to flow into the city.

The first flow was not too alarming. The lava was only slightly warm. It measured just 1 inch (2.5 centimeters) thick. But the next flow was merciless. Moving at nearly 50 miles (80 kilometers) per hour, a river of boiling lava rushed over Pompeii. It easily broke through the city walls that were built to protect its people from intruders. The burning slush of volcanic

Mount Vesuvius, Pompeii, Naples, and Herculaneum

ITALY

Herculaneum
PORTICI PALACE
MOUNT VESUVIUS
Naples
Pompeii (La Civitá)
Bay of Naples
Tyrrhenian Sea

N

0   5   10 mi
0   5   10   15 km

ITALY

Adriatic Sea

Miles
0   40   80   120
0   100   200
Kilometers

● Rome

MOUNT VESUVIUS
Naples

SARDINIA

Tyrrhenian Sea

N

Ionian Sea

SICILY

AFRICA

MEDITERRANEAN SEA

matter destroyed everything in its path. It covered the city and killed everyone left behind.

The next morning, only the tips of Pompeii's tallest buildings were visible. Vesuvius destroyed two other nearby towns, Herculaneum and Stabiae, that day. Roman historians wrote about the fate of Pompeii and the other two towns. But for centuries, the city and towns remained beneath the earth's surface. There they were untouched and frozen in time.

The Portici palace was built for Charles of Bourbon when he became king of the Two Sicilies in 1734. He hoped to decorate it with treasures found in Pompeii and Herculaneum

CHAPTER one

DISCOVERING HERCULANEUM

It's a summer day in 1738. Near the Italian town of Resina, a farmer is digging a well to water his fields. His shovel, with a heavy clunk, hits something. The farmer reaches into the loose dirt. He pulls a group of odd marble objects from the ground. The farmer wonders what his strange finds might be. He doesn't know that they are ancient treasures, buried here many centuries ago.

News of the farmer's discovery spreads across the Italian countryside. Soon it reaches Portici. At this seaside town, laborers are building a great palace, surrounded by beautiful gardens. The palace will be the summer home of Charles of Bourbon, the son of the king of Spain. Four years earlier, Charles took control of Naples and Sicily, two areas of present-day Italy. He declared himself king of the Two Sicilies.

Word of the farmer's finds reaches Charles. He is fascinated by the news of the strange discovery. He sends Colonel Rocque Joachin de Alcubierre, a member of his army, to find out more.

Charles of Bourbon *(above)* was the son of the king of Spain. Spain controlled the southern half of the Italian peninsula during the 1700s, and Charles named himself its king.

BENEATH RESINA

Alcubierre soon arrives in Resina. The locals tell him that this isn't the first time marble objects have been found in the ground. Over the years, many people digging wells have come upon similar items. In fact, the town proudly displays four marble torsos behind a church. According to the townspeople, they were discovered in the 1500s.

The people of Resina also tell Alcubierre about Maurice de Lorraine, Prince d'Elboeuf. D'Elboeuf came to Portici in 1709 to build a villa (a large house) by the sea. Like Charles, the prince heard about ancient statues found nearby. He began the first organized dig at Resina. D'Elboeuf hoped to find some beautiful pieces of carved marble to decorate his home.

D'Elboeuf's Museum

With a crew of eight diggers, Prince d'Elboeuf managed to bring in quite a haul at Resina. His men uncovered marble columns, portrait heads, and as many as eighteen life-size statues. D'Elboeuf proudly displayed the pieces at his villa. D'Elboeuf also sent a few statues to a cousin in Austria. The cousin later displayed them in Dresden, Germany. Charles's wife, Queen Maria Amalia (right), may have seen them there. If she did, Maria Amalia probably helped inspire Charles's interest in Resina.

Charles's wife, Maria Amalia of Saxony, was a German princess. This portrait was painted by a German artist, Anton Raffael Mengs in the 1700s.

Charles has other reasons for wanting to find more treasures. The pope (head of the Roman Catholic Church) lives in a palace in nearby Rome. Popes have displayed ancient objects as symbols of their power. As the new king of the Two Sicilies, Charles is eager to show off antiquities, rare old objects, of his own.

FINDING TREASURE

Working for the king, Alcubierre begins to explore Resina on October 22, 1738. Tunneling under the town, his small crew finds a marble statue on the very first day. The workers spend all night getting it out of the tunnel. As soon as they get it to the surface, Alcubierre orders his exhausted crew to carry it to Portici. At the palace, they set it up in the courtyard. Alcubierre wants it to be the first thing the king sees when he wakes up.

As the days pass, Alcubierre's crew keeps coming upon marvelous finds. They continue digging in the same area d'Elboeuf's men had. Soon they discover a theater building that is filled with marble and bronze statues. There they find

This model of the theater at Herculaneum was made in the 1920s. Alcubierre's crew tunneled into the theater in 1738 and found many treasures for the Portici palace.

an inscription reading "Theatrum Herculanensi." The inscription tells them two things. They are excavating ancient Herculaneum, and the building they are digging out was the town's theater.

By accident, the workers also come upon another building. It is Herculaneum's basilica. A basilica is a large public building used as a meetinghouse. At the basilica, Alcubierre finds walls decorated with fabulous paintings of figures from Greek and Roman mythology. They include the heroes Hercules and Theseus.

The king and the members of his court are particularly excited by the discovery of these wall paintings, or frescoes. Writings from ancient Rome mention paintings, but few paintings have survived. The frescoes at

Roman Frescoes

The walls of many Roman homes were decorated with wall paintings. They were usually painted using a technique called fresco. To paint a fresco, a Roman artist first covered a wall with plaster. While it was still wet, the artist painted it with pigments. These are colored paints made from ground-up minerals. Once the plaster dried, the brightly colored pigments were permanently fixed on the plaster walls.

Herculaneum has many frescoes that tell the story of Hercules (*figure on right in fresco at left*), the hero who, according to legend, founded the town.

> "[Visitors] are observed with greater jealousy and watchfulness since the scandalous behavior of some sharper [thieves], who have . . . pocket[ed] any small rarity upon which they could lay their hands."
>
> —painter John Russell, on visiting Portici in 1749

John Russell was a British portrait painter. He visited the Portici palace in 1749 to see the Roman treasures there.

Herculaneum are a rare find. They also provide a new key to understanding the art of Roman painting.

The walls with the paintings are chipped out of the buildings. They are carted to the Portici palace. At the palace, scholars in the king's court can study them. Soon the palace becomes a kind of museum. But the court is very choosy about who can view the treasures there. The king considers them his private property, to do with whatever he likes.

WELLS AND TUNNELS

Despite some success, the early days of the excavation are busy and difficult. Alcubierre is part of the problem. He was trained as a military engineer. He knows about mining techniques. But he has no background in excavating ancient ruins, and his approach to excavation is extremely haphazard. Each day he relies on his best hunch to decide where to dig next. All the while, he is driven by only one goal. He wants to get as many treasures out of the ground as fast and cheaply as possible. Alcubierre hopes filling the Portici palace with beautiful antiquities will win him the king's favor.

By trial and error, Alcubierre develops a system for digging beneath Resina. He designs a simple machine to help him. It uses existing wells to reach the ancient city below. Alcubierre has his crew attach a large net to a rope. The rope is then fixed to a winch. This is a device made from a large spool and a crank. By turning the crank one way, workers lower men inside the net into a well. By turning it the other way, they raise the net

By the early 1800s, crews at Herculaneum still worked in dark, narrow tunnels lit only by torches.

back up, carrying the men and—Alcubierre hopes—artifacts, or ancient objects, in it.

The workers inside the wells continue to dig deeper and deeper into the ground. If the well looks promising, they dig tunnels extending out from it. These new passages let them explore an even larger area. But the tunnels are very cramped. Most are only about 7 feet (2 m) high and

3 feet (1 m) wide. They are so narrow that the workers have to cut out places in the sides so they can pass one another. The tunnels are too deep for sunlight to reach them. All work has to be done by torchlight. The torches fill the tunnels with smoke. There is one good thing about his system. The workers can continue to dig day and night.

When Vesuvius erupted, Herculaneum was covered with boiling mud mixed with lava and ash. As it cooled, the mud became

This interior of a house at Herculaneum was not uncovered until a later time. Alcubierre was more interested in antiquities than in the buildings that house them.

very solid. As a result, Alcubierre's men must struggle to dig through it. Often the work is difficult and slow. Alcubierre is always desperate to make the next glorious find. If little is found in one tunnel, he quickly orders his men to move on to the next.

Each time the crew at Herculaneum digs a new tunnel, it faces another problem. What do they do with all the dirt they dig out? They take some to Portici. It is used to landscape the king's gardens there. But they dump most along the Royal Road in Resina. Soon the piles of dirt are so large they begin to block traffic.

Alcubierre has to come up with a better plan. He orders his men to dump dirt they dig from each new tunnel into an old one. The dirt reburies the remains of any buildings his men have found. But Alcubierre doesn't care about the buildings. He's only interested in large, precious objects that can be displayed at Portici. To him, the ancient structures his workers uncover are little more than storehouses for the treasure.

> "[Visitors will] find nothing but long narrow passages, just high enough to walk upright in, with a basket on the head, and wide enough for the workmen who carry them to pass each other with the dirt they dig out. There is a vast number of these passages, cut one out of another, so that one might perhaps walk the space of two miles [3 km]."
>
> —visitor to Herculaneum in 1751

The artist Camillo Paderni complained that the work crews at Herculaneum reburied or destroyed buildings and all objects that weren't suitable for Charles's collections. These

CHAPTER two

LEARNING TO EXCAVATE

Not everyone shares Alcubierre's interest in searching for great objects of art. Learning of the excavation, scholars studying ancient Rome flock to Resina. The court allows a few to tour the tunnels. Most are amazed by how chaotic the work sites are. They blame Alcubierre. They complain that both he and Charles are mere treasure hunters.

CRITICIZING THE EXCAVATION

Many of the scholars believe that Alcubierre's approach is too random. They are sure that the workers are missing important antiquities. They also complain about the objects taken to Portici. These objects are only the ones Alcubierre thinks are important. Many of the scholars don't think that Alcubierre is much good as an art expert. Among his critics is Camillo Paderni, an artist who visits the site in 1740. Paderni writes, "[I]f [Alcubierre's men] meet with any pieces of painting not so well preserved as the rest, they leave them where they are found. Besides, there are pillars of stucco extremely curious, consisting of many sides, all variously painted, of which they do not preserve the memory."

Other critics share Paderni's concern. They also feel that Alcubierre is not properly recording the sites of his discoveries. At the command of the royal court, Alcubierre is keeping a list of the objects found. But he's been slow to make plans—drawings of the areas excavated. These drawing would show walls, buildings, and streets. One visitor angrily notes that, without plans, it's impossible to get any real understanding of the layout of the ancient city. "[A]fter wandering some hours with torches," the visitor writes, "I cannot say I was able to form a distinct notion of the situation of the houses, streets, or anything, except of the theater, which was not again filled up. Such was the confusion that reigned everywhere!"

Hercules' City

The city of Herculaneum was named after the Greek mythological hero Heracles, who was known to the Romans as Hercules. According to legend, Hercules was the founder of Herculaneum.

Other scholars are upset that Alcubierre is filling in old tunnels. They want him to clear away the entire layer of volcanic matter covering Herculaneum. That way, they can study all artifacts, large and small, as they are uncovered. They will be able to see for themselves the layout of buildings and the city. They won't need Alcubierre's plans.

DANGER IN THE TUNNELS

Alcubierre's crew is far too small to do an open-air excavation of the whole buried town. As it is, even his present tunneling scheme is too much for his crew. As a military man, Alcubierre has no trouble driving his workers hard. The workers can't complain. Many of them are criminals, sentenced to hard labor for no pay. Alcubierre watches them closely to make sure no one escapes.

For the crew, their working conditions are even worse than Alcubierre's discipline. The tunnels, dug in a hurry, sometimes collapse. Workers are injured. After a tour of the tunnels, one visitor writes that "one cannot think oneself entirely secure from some fatal accident." Spending hours in the dark tunnels is physically hard on the workers. They breathe in the smoke from their torches and bits of volcanic dust. The tunnels are always damp. Every time it rains, they fill with water.

Not surprisingly, many crew members become ill. Alcubierre himself gets sick in November 1739. He has to give up his post for a month. When he returns the next year, he faces a new problem. While he was gone, a tunnel collapsed. His superiors wonder whether Alcubierre really knows what he is doing. They begin keeping a close eye on his work. This pressure makes Alcubierre's health problems worse. By mid-1741, he is suffering from exhaustion, blurry vision, and the disease scurvy. Once again, Alcubierre's health forces him to give up the excavation.

BARDET'S BATTLES

In July 1741, a French engineer named Pierre Bardet de Villeneuve takes Alcubierre's job. For the next four years, Bardet has his laborers working at a teriffic pace. He digs into many large public buildings, including the basilica. There he finds marble portrait statues of the Roman emperors Augustus, Claudius, and Titus.

Under Bardet, the excavation becomes even more chaotic. Adding to the problems is Bardet's prickly personality. He often fights with other officials involved in the excavation. He is a disaster in dealing with the residents of Resina. After years of digging, they have become tired of the excavation. It has disrupted their lives. Many of their houses are falling down. The tunnels dug under the town have weakened their foundations. In some areas, the ground has fallen into the tunnels. This has collapsed buildings and destroyed farm fields.

Pierre Bardet de Villeneuve and his crew found marble statues in the basilica, including this one of the Roman emperor Titus. Titus ruled from A.D. 79 to A.D. 81.

Whenever the townspeople complain, Bardet responds with utter contempt. On one occasion, he butts heads with a merchant named Sportullo. Bardet invites Sportullo to tour the tunnels. When Sportullo refuses, Bardet decides to teach him a lesson. He sends guards to bring him to the tunnel at bayonet point. Shaming Sportullo angers the townspeople. They complain to Bardet's superiors. After receiving reprimands from his supervisors, Bardet becomes fed up with his job. He repeatedly asks to leave his post. Finally, in 1745, he is replaced by Alcubierre, who is well enough to go back to work.

ALCUBIERRE RETURNS

Back at the Herculaneum site, Alcubierre makes some spectacular finds. His knowledge of engineering proves more useful than ever. After his men remove one large statue, he shows them how to quickly prop up the space it left. This helps prevent the collapse of the tunnel. In another case, his men find a statue, but it is in a very dusty area. Because of the dust, there's not enough oxygen to keep the torches burning. Alcubierre orders

An Angry Town

One day the crew at Resina sets off a near riot. They try to go down into a well, but a crowd of old women gathers around them. The women want to see what they are up to. Accidentally, the workers break the well. The women become so angry that the workers fear they will start throwing rocks at them. They pay the owner of the well some money for all the trouble they've caused. This helps calm the situation.

But by then, the entire town has turned out to see what is going on. The workers try to send a man down the well to explore. The townspeople are sure the man is going to be killed. They start yelling. The other workers are listening for shouts from the man below. They want to make sure he is still alive. But they cannot hear a thing over the noise of the crowd. Angry, some of the workers pull out their swords. They threaten to kill anyone who says another word. Suddenly, everyone is silent. The crew gets back to its work.

Alcubierre and his crew had to enlarge their tunnels and widen the access shaft to haul out this marble statue of Marcus Nonius Balbus on horseback.

his men to cut a hole into the area. Using a device of Alcubierre's design, the men then suck the dusty air out the hole and pump clean air in.

Among Alcubierre's most spectacular finds since he returns are two marble statues. They are of the Herculaneum official Marcus Nonius Balbus and his son, both on horseback. The huge statues stand about 8 feet (2.6 m) high. They are almost perfectly preserved. Their size, though, makes it impossible to get them through the tunnels. Alcubierre is desperate to get his hands on the statues. He orders his men to work for ten days straight. They open up old tunnels and widen the access shaft. They also build a special crate to haul up the statues. After many struggles, the workers manage to get them to the surface intact.

Alcubierre sometimes comes upon small private houses and shops. He doesn't have much interest in these. The small houses don't contain the

Later excavations in Herculaneum uncovered this small private house on a street called Cardo IV.

bronze and marble statues that the public buildings do. Ignoring these houses is not just his personal preference. He's also obeying the orders of the king's court. Alcubierre is supposed to record minor finds but send only major objects to Portici. There, each night, Charles is formally presented with the day's most marvelous discoveries.

Alcubierre is desperate to remain in Charles's favor. He is under constant pressure to find bigger and better finds. But after 1746, major discoveries are fewer. Convinced Herculaneum has no more valuable finds, Alcubierre starts looking elsewhere.

TO LA CIVITÁ

In early 1748, Alcubierre hears some promising news. Near the town of Torre Annunziata is an area known as La Civitá. Some land belonging to a farmer in La Civitá has caved in. In the hollow, the farmer finds remains of marble statues and paintings.

Excited by the news, Alcubierre contacts the prime minister in Naples. He asks for permission to move a few workers from Herculaneum to this new site. With a twelve-man crew, Alcubierre begins excavating La Civitá. As the digging begins, he is sure he's found the ancient town of Stabiae. Alcubierre is wrong about Stabiae. But he's right in thinking he's found something big. Unknown to Alcubierre, La Civitá rests atop the city of Pompeii.

Excavating Pompeii is much simpler than excavating Herculaneum. Unlike Herculaneum, Pompeii is not covered by hardened mud. Instead, it is buried under the lapilli. These small pieces of lava are fairly loose. Digging into them is relatively easy. Alcubierre sees that excavation there can go far faster with fewer workers. Also, the workers can get to the treasure by digging open trenches. They don't need to carve tunnels. This means they can work in daylight in fresh air.

But soon it's also clear the excavation is going to be expensive. Digging open trenches will destroy the area's farms and vineyards. To soothe angry landowners, the king has to pay a good price for the use of the land.

Proof of Pompeii

For the first few years, the workers at La Civitá do not know for sure what ancient city they are digging up. They finally find out by accident in 1763. They spy the words "Res Publica Pompeianorum" carved onto a wall. This phrase—the Romans' official name for the city of Pompeii—offers the first positive proof of where they are.

Digging at Pompeii proves very dangerous. Workers can easily fall into the trenches or slip into pits of loosened lapilli. Mofeta, pockets of gas trapped in the volcanic debris, are another threat. The gas released from the mofetas contains large amounts of poisonous carbon dioxide. If the workers dig into a mofeta and release the gas, breathing it can be deadly. The workers soon learn that when they hit a mofeta, a rotten-egg smell fills the air. The smell is made by the release of the gas hydrogen sulfide. Just a whiff of this foul odor sends workmen scrambling, fearing for their lives. Only weeks into the project, the site has to be shut down for three months to allow the gas-filled air to clear.

Alcubierre and his men finally get back to work. He is more eager than ever for an exciting find. He decides to dig up Pompeii's amphitheater. This is a great open-air arena where contests and spectacles were held. Alcubierre has no trouble finding the site. The outlines of the buried amphitheater seating can be seen on the surface. Alcubierre hopes Pompeii's amphitheater will be a treasure trove just as Herculaneum's theater was.

To Alcubierre's frustration, the site yields nothing for two months. He moves his men to the other side of the city. But even there, the new finds are few. After another mofeta scare, Alcubierre has had it. He abandons La Civitá altogether in search of more promising sites.

When Alcubierre went back to work at La Civitá, he began with the town's large amphitheater *(below)*. Its outline stood out on the modern surface of the town.

The J. Paul Getty Museum *(above)* in Malibu, California, was built as a replica of the Villa
of the Papyri near Herculaneum. Weber found this seafront villa in 1750.

CHAPTER three
WEBER'S MISSION

In 1749 Alcubierre is promoted to lieutenant colonel. His new rank comes with new duties. This means that he will have to spend more time in the capital city of Naples. Alcubierre reluctantly asks for an assistant. He recommends Karl Jakob Weber for the job.

ASSISTING ALCUBIERRE

Weber is a well-educated military engineer from Switzerland. He probably met Alcubierre during his six years as an engineer with the Royal Guard in Naples. Besides his engineering experience, Weber is fluent in Italian and Spanish. His Italian will let him speak directly with local residents and workers. His Spanish will help him report back to the court, which uses Spanish in official documents.

In July 1750, Weber reports for work. Alcubierre lays out a long list of instructions for him. He tells Weber to keep a close eye on all equipment and workers. Alcubierre is particularly concerned about workers trying to steal artifacts small enough to slip into a pocket. Alcubierre insists that Weber come down hard on any thieves. They are to be beaten and then sent to prison.

Alcubierre also instructs Weber to keep expenses within budget. He is to make weekly reports of all finds. Alcubierre makes it clear though that he alone will present these reports to the prime minister. Alcubierre has no trouble passing along responsibility to Weber. But he keeps for himself the credit for discoveries.

NEW DISCOVERIES

During his first two years on the job, Weber is very busy. He works at many different places in the area. The most promising is the Herculaneum site. Weber learns that in May 1750, a man drilling a well found some colored marble. Weber orders a crew there to dig a shaft deep into the ground. They burrow down 65 feet (20 m) before striking a large circular pavilion. Soon it's clear the pavilion is only a small part of a much greater discovery. It is an ancient grand villa that sits on a long stretch of seafront.

The site is a treasure trove. It is full of spectacular bronze and marble statues. Weber is just as excited by the floors of many of the rooms. They are covered with intricate mosaics. Mosaics are designs or pictures made from white, black, and multicolored tiles. The mosaics are beautiful works of art. Even more, they also help guide the excavation. By following the changes in floor decoration, Weber can follow one room to the next. He makes wonderful finds all along the way.

The number of large artifacts Weber finds is both a delight and a challenge. To get them safely to the surface, he has his workers build an extra-large access shaft. Weber also has to deal with another problem. While digging, his men keep coming upon old tunnels.

"[T]he sleeve of thick iron on the wheel broke—which no one could foresee since there were invisible and intrinsic cracks—and by a miracle I had enough time to be lifted from the well, and the supervisor and others congratulated me for having been reborn there."

—Karl Weber, on his near death in a tunnel, when a winch broke, 1752

Weber discovered many mosaic floors at Herculaneum. He was able to tell when he entered different rooms because the floor mosaic changed pattern. The swastika is found in many ancient cultures. It was often used as a sun symbol in Roman times.

No one is sure who dug them. They may have been made fairly recently. But without firm evidence, Alcubierre is sure they were dug by ancient Roman looters. He believes the thieves returned to Herculaneum after the volcanic debris cooled. They were looking for art and other objects.

Who dug the old tunnels is not that important to Weber. He is more worried about how to deal with them. He rightly fears the old tunnels could collapse with all the new digging around them. The old tunnels are also a fire hazard. In one incident, a fire breaks out when a worker's pick opens a tunnel full of sulfur gas. The gas

causes his lamp to explode. For their own protection, whenever his men find an old tunnel, Weber orders them to fill it in.

THE VILLA OF THE PAPYRI

Despite Weber's troubles, he is thrilled with the treasures of the villa. The most important is discovered in October 1752. It is a room filled with scrolls of charred papyrus. Papyrus is a plant material used in the ancient world to make paper. This library and its contents suggest a new name for the house: the Villa of the Papyri. (Papyri is the plural of papyrus.)

News of the scrolls travels through Europe. Scholars scramble to learn more. They are desperate to find out what's written in these ancient books. Charles's court tries to satisfy them. He brings a priest named Antonio Piaggio to Naples to unroll the scrolls and read the text.

Piaggio gets down to work. At the same time, Camillo Paderni boasts of his role in retrieving the scrolls. Paderni is a scholar at Portici. Charles had placed him in charge of studying the discoveries and drawing images

Piso's Library

Years after Weber's excavation of the Villa of the Papyri, scholars learned who built this grand house. His name was Lucius Calpurnius Piso Caesoninus. His daughter, Calpurnia, was married to Julius Caesar, a famous and powerful Roman ruler of the first century b.c. Piso was a well-educated man. His great library included more than eighteen hundred scrolls. It is the largest ancient library ever discovered.

of them. He writes a letter to the Royal Society of London, Great Britain's most famous science academy. In the letter, he claims responsibility for the find. He writes, "I was buried . . . for more than twelve days, to carry off the volumes found there; many of which were so perished, that it was impossible to remove them."

Piaggio, though, uncovers a different story when he interviews those involved in the discovery. He finds out that many of the papyri were destroyed by the workers. At first, they thought the papyri were just pieces of wood. Then they noticed the objects were all the same size. Out of curiosity, they began to unroll them. The workers still could not figure out what they were. But they did know the papyri were not the statues and marbles the king wanted most.

Through his detective work, Piaggio concludes that Weber

The original bronze statue of a boy (right) found in the Villa of the Papyri is in the National Archaeological Museum in Naples, Italy. A copy stands in the Villa of the Papyri.

saved the scrolls. Weber saw the workers throwing away the paper. He demanded they stop. According to Piaggio, Paderni exaggerated his role in the discovery. In reality, he was in part responsible for the destruction of many of the scrolls. He was the one who had encouraged the workers to ignore everything but major finds.

FIGHTING FOR RECOGNITION

These finds at the Villa of the Papyri make Weber feel he's doing a good job. It's time, he thinks, for the court to reward him for his good work. In 1752 Weber writes a letter to the prime minister. He asks for an increase in his budget. He also suggests he get a promotion to lieutenant colonel. This is the same rank held by Alcubierre. Weber carefully makes his case. He points out that the objects from the villa are worth a fortune. Increasing the excavation budget, then, is a good investment. The promotion seems reasonable, he writes, considering the dangers he faces every day in the mines.

The prime minister, though, is not convinced. He flatly refuses all Weber's requests. It is likely that Alcubierre is behind the refusal. Alcubierre began to turn on Weber soon after Weber became his assistant. He's convinced that Weber is a social climber, just using his job to try to rise above his place. Alcubierre is always conscious of his own social position. He is appalled that Weber dared to ask for a rank equal to his. Alcubierre also becomes furious when he learns that Weber has asked for a carriage. Weber claims that riding a horse from site to site is ruining his clothing. Alcubierre is sure the real reason Weber wants a carriage is so he can pose as a nobleman.

"[T]he excavators began to observe a quantity of fragments resembling carbonized [burned] wood, and when every trace of this timber was found, and these papyri resembled nothing more than wood . . . they were disregarded and left in the earth without anyone's thinking twice."

—Antonio Piaggio, writing in 1753 about the discovery of scrolls in the Villa of the Papyri

"The great bronze statue of the Roman woman found in the theater, how much would it cost? . . . [T]he marble vase; . . . the candelabra, all of bronze; all the paintings, of which there are very many quite good and rare. Just to make these objects anew would cost a small treasure! But since they are antiquities, nearly 2,000 years old or more, for their verification and restitution to the historical sciences they are worth a great fortune."

—Karl Weber , 1752

This marble statue of a woman was found in the theater in Herculaneum. It may be the one that Weber refers to in his request (at left) for a promotion and an increase in his budget.

Alcubierre is also annoyed by Weber's working methods. Without Alcubierre's permission, Weber is experimenting with new excavation techniques. For instance, he tries leaving all the tunnels open, instead of refilling them with debris. This way, he does not run the risk of accidentally excavating the same area twice. To keep the open tunnels from collapsing, his men prop them up with wooden beams or stone pillars. Weber finally gives up this plan though. The extra workers he needs are very expensive. Also, Weber realizes the beams and pillars do little good. Even when they are in place, the tunnels still might collapse.

Alcubierre has another reason for being angry at Weber. Weber has not produced a plan of the villa. When Alcubierre was the hands-on director of the excavation, he was lazy about drawing plans. But he's under pressure to present one to the king.

"[A]t the time when I had to name an engineer to oversee the excavations under my direction, I inclined [leaned] toward [Weber], having believed with certainty on that occasion that he would have the knowledge through his engineering work in Naples and that he would be the best for such a duty. My experience since then, however, has shown me that his presence has served me little in those tasks, and more recently he has altered on several occasions the manner in which matters have been carried out in the past."

—Rocque Joachin de Alcubierre, 1751

Weber has a good excuse. He tells Alcubierre he can't possibly draw a plan until the excavation of the villa is finished. Alcubierre, though, is not impressed. He keeps nagging his assistant.

Finally in 1754, after four years of work, Weber finishes his plan. Weber's drawing of the site contains several mistakes, but overall it's an excellent record. He takes care to list all the important finds. Then he fits them into the plan, showing where each object was discovered. He adds facts about the excavation and offers guesses about how the Romans used different rooms in the house.

THE ACCADEMIA ERCOLANESE

Weber is not the only one struggling to record the excavation. Years earlier, the court decided to present its new collection of antiquities in a series of illustrated books. Ottavio Bayardi, a cousin of the prime minister, was hired to write these volumes. His annual salary was ten times what Weber earned.

In 1752 five books by Bayardi are published. The king and court hope the books will impress the world with their important discoveries. Instead, scholars throughout Europe ridicule Bayardi and his work. In 2,678 pages, Bayardi babbles on and on. He only briefly covers the one subject his readers are interested in—the antiquities themselves.

The court removes Bayardi from his post. In 1755 it establishes the Accademia Ercolanese (Academy of Herculaneum). The accademia includes fifteen of Naples's finest scholars. They are responsible for figuring out how to present the king's collection in official publications. They never think of consulting Weber, even though he is the single best source of information about what's been found.

Weber found sixteen white pillars when he excavated in a farmer's field in La Civitá.
Columns decorated many large public buildings, such as these at the basilica, in the
Roman city of Pompeii.

CHAPTER four

EXPLORING
POMPEII

Workers continue the excavation of the Villa of the Papyri. But Alcubierre orders Weber back to La Civitá in April 1755. There, a farmer has recently found a white marble pillar in his field. Excavating the spot, Weber discovers fifteen more in just a few days. Though Weber doesn't realize it, he is beginning the first large-scale excavation of the ancient city of Pompeii.

WORKING IN THE OPEN AIR

Weber digs through the loose lapilli at Pompeii. He finds it far easier than through the hard mud at Herculaneum, just as Alcubierre had. In a few years' time, he's able to uncover a large area, including a number of buildings. His crew moves to new areas without covering over old ones. This allows them to work faster. The system, however, presents some problems. The laborers have to remove objects they find as fast as they can. Otherwise, they could be destroyed by rain or sunlight. Antiquities left out in the open also attract thieves. Weber has to post guards at night. They make sure no one sneaks onto the site and takes valuable items. During the day, the crew foreman carries a gun so he can chase away any suspicious characters.

This fresco was found in a villa near Pompeii during an excavation there in the 1800s. This scene is part of a nine-paneled fresco depicting a ritual involving Dionysus *(not shown)*, the Roman god of wine. Experts disagree on the meaning of the fresco.

The site is full of treasures. In addition to fine statues, there are many wall paintings. These are so well preserved that they must have been made just before Vesuvius erupted. The paintings include several wonderful friezes—paintings in a horizontal band along the upper part of a wall. One shows an Egyptian scene, with figures and animals along the Nile River. Another depicts everyday life in the forum, Pompeii's public square.

To Weber, though, a much more exciting discovery lies in front of the buildings. There, he finds paved streets with a public fountain marking an intersection. He also starts exploring a few small private homes. As he expects, he doesn't find any valuable art there. But he's intrigued to find that most of the common household objects he comes upon are located in little rooms. Here is evidence of a Roman custom the ancients wrote about. Average Romans generally tucked away household items in a storeroom when they weren't in use.

Weber is also delighted to find a few small shops. He identifies counters that ancient store owners had used to display their wares. While digging through the site, Weber always enjoys finding parallels between ancient and modern times. For instance, in his notes, he writes that Pompeii's streets were paved with blocks of lava just as the streets of Naples are.

In Pompeii, Weber uncovered paved streets and public fountains, such as the one on the left below. He became interested in the way ordinary ancient Romans lived.

The House of Julia Felix faced the main street. Weber was intrigued by the inscriptions on the house's wall. They turned out to be advertisements and political campaign notices.

THE HOUSE OF JULIA FELIX

On one building facing the main street, Weber finds a number of painted inscriptions. Although he can read Latin—the language of the ancient Romans—he has trouble making out what the writings say. The wall will be cut down and moved to Portici. But before it is, Weber quickly copies the inscriptions so they can be studied by historians.

The scholars find that the inscriptions are actually public notices. Several are political advertisements for candidates for local elections. One large inscription turns out to be an advertisement saying parts of the building—including shops, baths, and second-story apartments—are available for rent. The building complex becomes known as the House of Julia Felix. This is the owner's name given in the advertisement.

Weber is also careful to gather small objects from private houses that can shed light on everyday Roman life. He finds fruits, nuts, eggs, and

Weber collected preserved food items at Pompeii. A fresco *(left)* shows a baker selling the same kinds of loaves of bread as those found in the ruins *(below)*.

loaves of bread—all perfectly preserved. The Portici museum exhibits some of the most spectacular antiquities ever found in the area. But these preserved foods become one of the most talked-about displays there.

HOPING FOR A GRAND DISCOVERY

Digging at Pompeii continues. But in 1756, Weber shifts his focus back to Herculaneum. He is sure that there are still treasures to be discovered at that site. Days and days pass. The work is slow, and little is found. As Alcubierre becomes impatient, Weber assures him he has a plan. Weber says he's going to follow the streets. That way, he's bound to come upon some buildings. He writes, "[B]y means of the layout of these streets, all the temples and buildings and everything inside them will be encountered, and one will know where he is going."

But this plan doesn't pay off. For months Weber finds nothing. Finally, his men unearth a small bronze statue of Venus, the Roman goddess of

An Exciting Find

At La Cività, workers found a small painted panel. It shows objects associated with Dionysus, the Roman god of wine. The find may have seemed minor, except for its historical importance. Centuries before, the Roman architect Vitruvius wrote that Roman home-owners often cut down old beloved wall paintings. They then framed them in wood or set them into the wet stucco of new walls. For scholars, finding the painted panel confirms Vitruvius's ancient writings.

love. Weber is excited. He is sure that it's just the first of many more discoveries to come. But Alcubierre is not so hopeful. In Portici, Paderni is also concerned. A workman tells him he's never seen a worse site. Losing confidence in the excavation, Paderni writes that Weber "would like to be an antiquarian [an expert in ancient art] when he is not one."

Weber ignores his critics. He keeps excavating the same area. He is convinced he'll discover a temple full of exciting objects. Here and there, Weber makes some small finds. He unearths a well-preserved statue of Hygeia, the Roman goddess of health. He also discovers a few beautiful objects made from solid gold and a bronze statuette of Hercules. But by late 1758, Alcubierre loses all patience. He tells Weber to move on. Alcubierre sends him to the area where Alcubierre found the paintings of Theseus and Hercules years before.

When Weber finds nothing there, he moves to a new area. He is still

"Can Your Excellency [Charles] believe that such objects improve by being handled by people who understand nothing? . . . [Weber is] tireless [and] serves the king well, yet he diminishes his merit through the obstinacy of his wicked brain."

—Camillo Paderni, complaining about Weber, 1757

A Golden Bulla

At Herculaneum in 1758, Weber's crew found a beautiful gold bulla. Roman children wore a bulla around their necks to ward off evil spirits and bring good luck. Most bullas were made out of cotton or leather. A bulla made from gold was fairly rare. The owner of the golden bulla from Herculaneum was probably from a very wealthy family.

This gold bulla excavated at Pompeii is similar to the one Weber's crew found in Herculaneum.

searching for a temple. He accidentally comes upon a network of tunnels dug long ago by Alcubierre's substitute, Pierre Bardet de Villeneuve. But he finds little else. Even so, Weber remains enthusiastic. He is convinced the next big find is just around the corner. By the end of 1759, Weber has spent more than four years excavating in Pompeii and Herculaneum. He has little to show for it. For all his efforts, Weber has found fewer than twenty pieces that the court felt were suitable for Charles's collection.

Mount Vesuvius looms over still uncovered ruins at modern-day Pompeii.

CHAPTER five

A PROPOSAL FOR THE ACCADEMIA

In 1759 Charles of Bourbon is called to Spain. He is to become king. As King Charles III of Spain, he lives far away from his Portici palace. He will no longer pay close attention to what is happening in Pompeii and Herculaneum. But he wants to show his continued interest in the excavations. He removes from his finger a ring that had been recovered in Pompeii. He's worn it for years, but he wants it to stay forever in Naples. Even as the king of Spain, he refuses to remove any objects from Portici. At Portici they can be preserved and studied.

WEBER'S PLAN

Charles places Bernardo Tanucci, his prime minister, in charge of the excavations. Within days, Weber comes to Tanucci with a proposal. The proposal includes twenty-nine plans of the

Charles returned to Spain to become King Charles III. This portrait of the king by Spanish painter Andres de la Calleja was made in 1759.

excavations he's worked on for almost ten years. He hopes the plans will get him appointed to the Accademia Ercolanese.

Weber tells Tanucci of his goal. He wants to persuade the accademia to make a big change in how it publishes information about the excavations. Up until then, the accademia has published images and descriptions of discoveries by type. That is, they group all statues together, all wall

Mount Vesuvius erupted again in November 1760. This painting from 1771 by Englishman William Hamilton shows local people and tourists visiting the site.

paintings together, and so on. Weber has a better idea. He wants to devote entire books to one site or even just one building. The books will include plans showing exactly where each object was found. To Weber this will help readers put the objects in context. From his books, they could get an idea of how Romans used their living spaces. They could also learn why Romans constructed buildings the way they did. The books would show

how Roman architecture reflected the ways the ancient Romans lived.

Applying to join the accademia is a brave move for Weber to make. After all, the accademia is made up of the greatest scholars in Naples. Weber has a solid education, but he isn't a nobleman. He also doesn't have the scholarly background expected of an accademia member.

In September 1760, Weber meets with the accademia to make his case. He shows them his plans and notebooks and outlines his publishing program. The accademia members are polite. They praise his efforts. But they refuse to admit him. They also dislike his ideas about how to organize books about the excavations. The members write, "The more natural method [is] . . . to avoid the confusion that would arise from Weber's method of mixing the paintings with the bronzes, marbles, medals, and inscriptions. Such things distinguished by class and published in separate volumes are more successful in conforming to the pleasure and taste of [educated] men." The type of book Weber imagines will not be published for decades.

FINDING DIANA

Weber is disappointed. He also has to accept the fact that none of the excavation sites are yielding much. Then, in November 1760, Vesuvius suddenly erupts. For fifty days, the volcano rumbles, disrupting work at the Villa of the Papyri for months.

"[Near where the Diana statue was found, there must be] palaces of some consideration—gardens, other buildings, columns, porticoes [columned porches], baths, most noble pavements—where one can hope for statues, fountains, and paintings, all well preserved because they are covered in dry lapilli, and because this is a site with a marvelous view of the sea."

—Karl Weber, 1760

Weber found a small statue of Diana at Pompeii. Later, archaeologists discovered this fresco of the Roman goddess of the hunt there.

Even when all the sites are running again, there are few major finds. One exception is a small marble statue of the Roman goddess Diana found in Pompcii. The Romans decorated their statues with paint. The Diana is so well preserved that much of its original yellow, blue, pink, and black paint is still on the statue.

The find lifts Weber's spirits. He's sure the area where the statue is found will be a good one. Like the Villa of the Papyri, it is located along the water. Weber reasons that the Diana statue must be from another seaside villa, rich with artifacts.

FRUSTRATION BUILDS

Weber has another reason to want to work in Pompeii. Paderni has begun to directly supervise the digging at the villa in Herculaneum. Weber is all too familiar with Paderni's personality. He is eager to stay as far away from him as possible. In Herculaneum, Paderni quickly gets a reputation for being demanding. He also is disrespectful of his workers. Paderni proves to be lazy too. He decides that Portici's storerooms are too full. He tells his work crews to use their pickaxes to smash any paintings he thinks are unworthy of the museum. Hearing that Paderni is destroying art, the king commands him to stop it immediately.

In Pompeii, over the next few months, Weber finds only a few promising items. His men unearth a gold earring in the shape of a chestnut. They also come upon a cameo. A cameo is a small carving in stone, ivory, or shell, usually set against a stone of a different color. This one showed the head of Minerva,

William Hamilton, who painted the Vesuvius eruption, drew this scene of the excavation at Pompeii in 1776.

> "Perhaps some four months of expense were worth an agate cameo, very well preserved and flawless. . . . It is not unique, because there are others like it in the museums of sovereigns [rulers], but it is most beautiful, and the agate is . . . [a] very rare type."
>
> —Prime Minister Bernardo Tanucci, 1761

At Pompeii, Weber found a cameo, like this one, engraved with a portrait of Minerva, the Roman goddess of wisdom.

the Roman goddess of wisdom. Perhaps with some exaggeration, Weber claims the cameo alone is "worth twenty statues."

These finds, however exciting, aren't nearly enough to satisfy Prime Minister Tanucci. He has to write weekly updates to the king. In these letters, he sounds more and more desperate as fewer antiquities are found. In March 1761, he writes, "The excavations have produced nothing this week, 'not even a nail,' as Paderni says." A few months later, Tanucci seems in despair: "[A]ll is bleak, all languid, all sterile, desolate, half alive."

This French plate from 1856 is part of a set with Pompeiian designs for the border and a center image based on an engraving of a treasure from Herculaneum. The European interest in Pompeii was still strong almost one hundred years after the first excavations there.

CRITICISM AND PRAISE

Bernardo Tanucci is not the only one who's upset. Paderni, Alcubierre, and Weber all are anxious about the situation. Soon they begin taking it out on one another.

Paderni says it's Alcubierre and Weber's fault. He insists to Tanucci that the two men are "in the dark in searching for the ancient monuments, as they lack the skill and necessary experience." Outraged that Weber dared to apply to the accademia, Alcubierre places the blame squarely on him. He calls for Weber's dismissal. Weber reacts to Alcubierre's attacks with bitterness and hurt. He replies "I deserve thanks rather than condemnation."

Johann Joachim Winckelmann (above), a German art historian, was not allowed to see all the treasures at the Portici palace and published his complaints. He later visited the dig sites and found more to complain about.

WINCKELMANN IN PORTICI

The excavators continue to turn on one another. Suddenly they face blistering criticism from an unexpected source—German scholar Johann Joachim Winckelmann. Winckelmann is an

A Practical Joke

In October 1761, Weber discovered a bronze horse and sent word of it to Alcubierre. Always desperate for the court's approval, Alcubierre raced to the Portici palace with the news. With much fanfare, Alcubierre announced the great find, which he assumed was a life-size statue. But actually, the horse is just miniature—a fact Weber conveniently neglected to mention. Weber's practical joke worked perfectly. A horrified Alcubierre learned that the fabulous find he had heralded at the court is the size of a toy. Alcubierre retaliated swiftly, spreading the untrue allegation that Weber was "always drunk morning and night."

expert in ancient art. Years earlier he had come to Naples to view the royal collection at Portici. He was not pleased by the reception he received. The court allowed him to see some pieces. But they would not give him complete access to the museum. The accademia members didn't want Winckelmann writing about the collection.

Annoyed, Winckelmann wrote that the sculptures he saw were "part mediocre, part bad." He had even harsher words for Paderni. He called him "a lousy draftsman who, to save himself from starvation in Rome, had the good fortune of being allowed to draw the ancient paintings. . . . This man is as much an impostor as he is a nitwit and an ignoramous and passes himself off as a Doctor of Antiquity."

Despite this disastrous visit, Winckelmann returns to Portici in 1762. This is just as the excavations have taken a turn for the worse. Paderni seems unaware of Winckelmann's nasty words about him. He befriends the scholar and lets him see the entire collection. Winckelmann is also permitted to visit the site in Pompeii where Weber found the Diana statue. He is allowed to review Weber's site plans. This time, Winckelmann comes away with a much better appreciation for the treasures that have been found.

Just as the accademia fears, Winckelmann writes about his journey in a letter to a friend. The letter is then widely published in Europe. In it Winckelmann discusses the sites and the objects in the museum. But his strongest opinions are reserved for the excavation itself. Winckelmann complains that too much energy is being spent on Herculaneum. Pompeii, he declares, is a better site. In his opinion, uncovering small private houses is a waste of time that can be better spent in search of villas. And he grumbles about the shortage of laborers. At the rate they're going, he complains, it will take four generations to excavate the sites.

Winckelmann's most stinging criticisms, however, are of the mismanagement of the sites. He's particularly hard on Alcubierre. Winckelmann calls him a mere "land surveyor," who was "as

This statue of Diana is in the Temple of Apollo (the Roman god of music and poetry) in Pompeii. The temple was the type of site Winckelmann approved of excavating because it was an important building.

By the late 1800s, Pompeii was a major tourist attraction. This interest had been predicted by the Naples ambassador to France. He suggested publishing a guide to the sites. Caroline, the sister of Napoleon, ruler of France, promoted the publication of the first guides to Pompeii in the early 1800s.

familiar with antiquities as the moon is with crabs." About the only person Winckelmann praises is Weber. "To this intelligent man," Winckelmann writes, "are owed all the sensible arrangements made [in the excavations.]" He compliments Weber's plans but adds that because of the court's secrecy, "these plans . . . are shown to no one."

AN EXCAVATOR'S END

Winckelmann's letter is published in Paris, France. Ferdinando Galiani, Naples's ambassador to France, quickly forwards a copy to Prime Minister

Tanucci. Along with it, he sends a recommendation. France's fascination with the excavation has sparked a craze. Wealthy French people are clamoring for everything in the "Herculaneum fashion." To meet this demand, painters, jewelers, and upholsterers are using ancient designs and images in their wares. Galiani urges Tanucci to take advantage of the Herculaneum mania. He suggests publishing a guide to the sites for foreign tourists.

Tanucci dismisses the idea. The court has its own plan for publishing its discoveries, and a tourist guide hardly fits in. As he writes Galiani, "Europe is not all French, that part which is not French asks for order: that is, all the paintings, all the statues, all the vases, and everything arranged in its own series."

"In this way the lifeless city would be reborn, and after one thousand seven hundred years see the light of day again. As a result we would learn many, many things about daily life, architecture, art and erudition [learning] that we seek in vain from books. With the greatest profit for the area, all of learned Europe will run to Naples, since they could not imagine anything more gratifying than to see with their own eyes the houses, basilicas, and temples."

—scholar Scipione Maffei, 1747,
on open-air excavations such as Pompeii

Tanucci rejects Galiani's proposal, but another idea for the sites begins to gain favor. For years many scholars have called for open-air excavations. This would make it easier for visitors to view the layout of buildings and streets. By the early 1760s, the Pompeii workers have stopped filling in unearthed areas. But the tunnels in Herculaneum are still being filled in. This is in part because working farms and vineyards otherwise would be destroyed.

Weber was initially against open-air excavations there. But finally, he warms to the idea. He becomes obsessed with creating an accurate plan of Herculaneum's theater. Day after day, he spends hours in its dark, dank tunnels. Over time, it becomes clear to him that he'll never learn enough about a site until it is completely uncovered. In 1763 he presents a detailed proposal to begin exposing Herculaneum's theater to the open air. The proposal is forwarded to the king.

Before Weber receives the go-ahead, he suddenly falls ill. The diagnosis is unclear. Possibly he suffers from silicosis, a lung disease caused by breathing in volcanic dust. He asks for a leave of absence to recover. He hopes to get back to Herculaneum as soon as possible. But to everyone's shock, Weber dies in Naples on February 15, 1764. A few months later, Winckelmann pays tribute to Weber and his work. He notes, "[W]e are obligated to the inexhaustible zeal [energy] of the chief engineer, Karl Weber." This very zeal, which furthered the Western world's understanding of antiquity, also likely cost Weber his life.

Herculaneum was exposed to open air after Weber died. In this photo, the modern city of Ercolano rises above the ancient town.

In this print from the 1800s, Guiseppe Fiorelli, the director of excavations in 1860, reads while his work crew uncovers more of Pompeii.

Epilogue

After Weber's death, the excavations of Pompeii and Herculaneum continued under Francesco La Vega. He was only twenty-seven at the time. La Vega studied all Weber's plans and notes to learn about his excavation techniques. When Alcubierre died in 1780, La Vega took over his job. He later became the director of the Museum Herculanense in Portici.

European scholars kept a close watch on how the excavations were going. Their interest sparked neoclassicism. This was a movement in art and architecture based on styles from the ancient Greek and Roman worlds. Construction of the White House in Washington, D.C., began during this period, in 1792. It is an example of the neoclassical style in architecture of the late 1700s.

In the 1800s, more and more people began visiting the excavation sites. Wealthy young Americans and Europeans considered a trip to Pompeii a necessary part of their education. An entire industry grew up around books that would guide them through the ancient ruins.

By then the excavations had become much more organized than they were in Alcubierre's day. Like Weber, later excavators were not just interested in finding treasure. They wanted to find out about how the Romans lived. In the 1800s and 1900s, the careful work of Giuseppe Fiorelli, Pietro

La Vega Vincenzo Spinazzola, and Amedeo Maiuri made great contributions to the world's understanding of these ancient sites. At the same time, they helped develop and further the science of archaeology. This new science established standards and techniques for excavation unknown in Weber and Alcubierre's day.

Pompeii is one of the best known and most visited sites in the world.

But its story is far from complete. When Vesuvius erupted in A.D. 79, the city stretched across 163 acres (66 hectares). But as of the early 2000s, only 66 acres (27 hectares) have been excavated *(below)*. The work continues in the twenty-first century. As the excavations go on, the site will no doubt yield new treasures and revelations. It will continue to build a bridge between the ancient world and modern times.

SELECTED SITES OF ANCIENT POMPEII

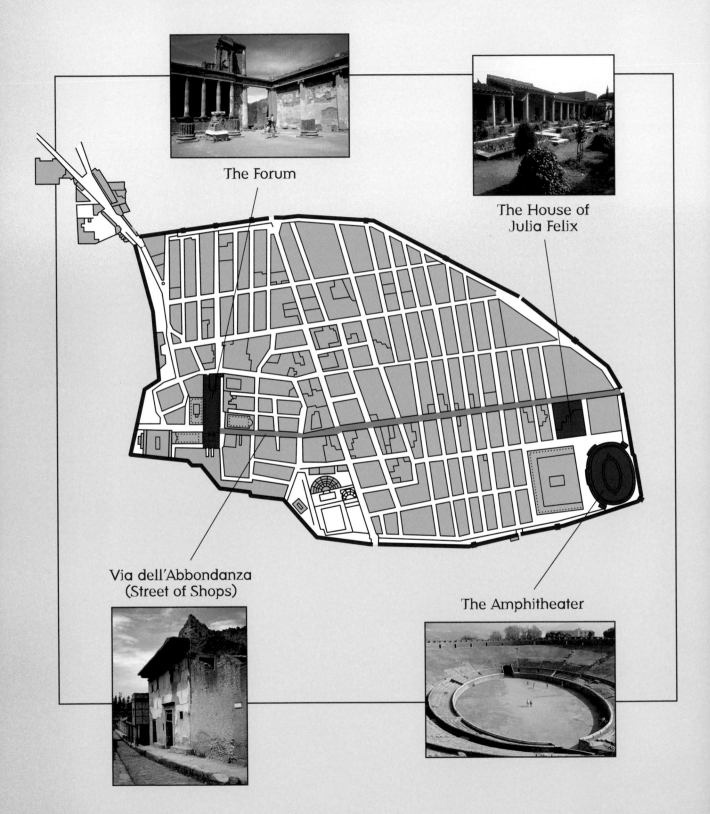

The Forum

The House of
Julia Felix

Via dell'Abbondanza
(Street of Shops)

The Amphitheater

EXCAVATION DATES

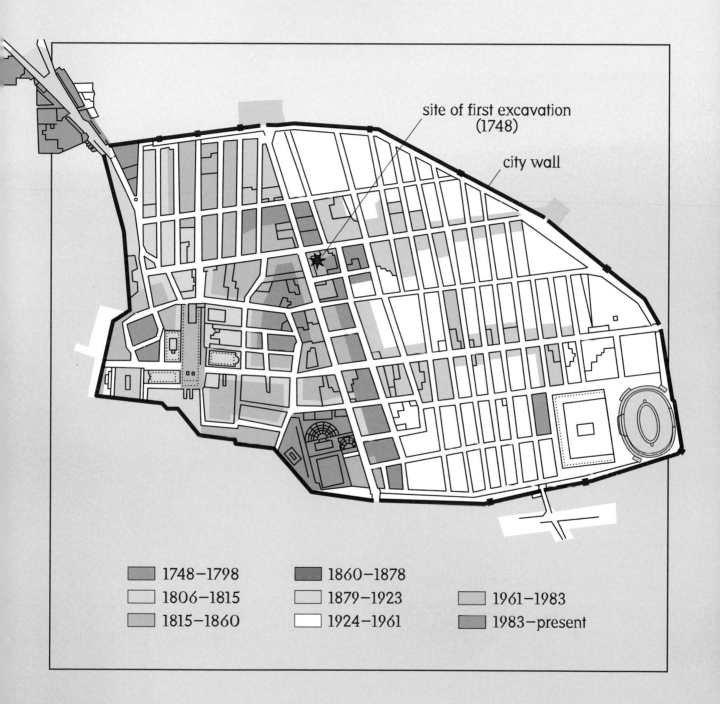

site of first excavation
(1748)

city wall

1748–1798	1860–1878	
1806–1815	1879–1923	1961–1983
1815–1860	1924–1961	1983–present

TIMELINE

6TH CENTURY B.C.
The city of Pompeii is founded by the Osci people of central Italy.

80 B.C.
Pompeii surrenders to Roman troops led by Lucius Cornelius Sulla. It becomes a Roman town.

A.D. **62**
Much of Pompeii is damaged by an earthquake.

79
The eruption of Mount Vesuvius destroys Pompeii and Herculaneum.

1709
Prince d'Elboeuf begins an informal excavation at Resina (ancient Herculaneum).

1734
Charles of Bourbon becomes king of the Two Sicilies (Naples and Sicily).

1738
Serious excavation of Herculaneum begins. The work is overseen by Rocque Joachin de Alcubierre and paid for by Charles of Bourbon.

1748
Excavation at La Cività (later identified as Pompeii) begins.

1750
Karl Jakob Weber is hired as Alcubierre's assistant. He takes over the day-to-day supervision of excavation sites.

1752
The library at the Villa of the Papyri in Herculaneum is discovered.

1755
The Accademia Ercolanese is founded.

1759
Charles of Bourbon leaves Naples to become Charles III, king of Spain.

1762
German scholar Johann Joachim Winckelmann publishes a letter criticizing the excavation of Pompeii and Herculaneum.

1763

Discovery of a sign proves that the La Cività site is the ancient city of Pompeii.

1764

Karl Weber dies in Naples.

1780

Francesco La Vega becomes director of excavations.

1860

The Italian states unite to form the country of Italy. Giuseppe Fiorelli becomes director of excavations.

1863

Fiorelli develops a technique to make plaster casts of bodies in Pompeii.

1910

Vincenzo Spinazzola becomes director of excavation. He begins to excavate both sides of Via dell'Abbondanza, the street of shops.

1924

Amadeo Maiuri becomes director of excavation.

1927

Vesuvius erupts for many months.

1944

Vesuvius erupts again.

1957

The Museo Archeologico Nazionale (National Archaeological Museum) is founded in Naples to house the treasures from Pompeii and Herculaneum.

2000 AND BEYOND

Excavations continue at Pompeii and Herculaneum.

PRONUNCIATION GUIDE

The people of Pompeii and Herculaneum spoke Latin. This ancient language is rarely used in modern times. But many contemporary languages are based on Latin. They include Spanish, Italian, and French. These are called Romance languages, since they are derived from the language of ancient Rome.

Below is a pronunciation key to the Latin and Italian names used in the text:

Accademia Ercolanese	ah-ka-dah-MEE-ah ehr-koh-lah-NAYZ-ee
Rocque Joachin de Alcubierre	ROOK wah-KEEN duh ahl-KEW-bee-ayr
Dionysus	DY-oh-ny-suhs
Herculaneum	hehr-kew-LAYN-ee-uhm
Hygeia	HY-gee-eh
Lucius Calpurnius Piso Caesoninus	LEW-shuhs kal-PUR-nee-uhs PEES-so say-SOH-nee-nuhs
Marcus Nonius Balbus	MAR-kus NOHN-ee-uhs BAL-buhs
Pompeii	pahm-PAY or pahm-PAY-y
Portici	pohr-TEE-chee
Theseus	THEE-see-uhs
Titus	TY-tuhs
Vesuvius	veh-SOO-vee-uhs
Vitruvius	vih-TROO-vee-uhs

GLOSSARY

amphitheater: a round structure with tiers of seats surrounding a central arena

ancient: relating to a time long ago, particularly before the fall of the Roman Empire in A.D. 476

antiquity: an object, especially a work of art, made during ancient times

archaeology: the recovery and study of buildings, tools, pottery, and other objects used by humans in the past

basilica: an ancient Roman public building that was used as a meetinghouse

cameo: a carving in shell, ivory, or stone, often of a person's profile, set against a stone of a different color

excavation: the process of exposing something by digging it up

forum: the public square of an ancient Roman city

lapilli: small pieces of solid lava

mofeta: an opening in the earth out of which gases, such as carbon dioxide, escape

mosaic: a decorative design or picture made from small pieces of stone or tile

papyrus: a kind of paper made from the papyrus plant. This paper was first used in ancient Egypt.

pavilion: an ornamental structure in a garden, sometimes used for entertainment or for shelter

stucco: a fine plaster used to cover interior walls, or a harder material to cover exterior walls

villa: a large country house

winch: a machine used to lift heavy objects

WHO'S WHO?

Alcubierre, Rocque Joachin de (1702–1780) A Spanish army engineer who arrived in Naples with Charles of Bourbon. Alcubierre's army training made him an expert in tunneling methods, but he had no training in archaeology. His main concern was to find treasure to decorate the king's palace.

Bardet de Villeneuve, Pierre (1700s) This French engineer took charge of the digs in 1741 when Alcubierre became ill. His contempt for the local people caused him problems.

Bayardi, Ottavio (1690–1765) A cousin of the prime minister of Naples, Bayardi was brought in to write a series of books about the finds at Pompeii and Herculaneum. The books were published beginning in 1752 and ridiculed throughout Europe. Bayardi was removed from his position.

Charles of Bourbon (1716–1788) The son of the king of Spain. He took control of the Naples area in 1734 and named himself king of the Two Sicilies. Charles sponsored the digs at Pompeii and Herculaneum to acquire antiquities for his palace at Portici. He later became Charles III of Spain.

Lorraine, Maurice de, Prince d'Elboeuf (1677–1763) A prince who built a villa at Portici in 1709. He organized the first dig at Resina after hearing about ancient statues found nearby.

Maria Amalia (1724–1760) As the wife of King Charles, she may have seen statues found by Prince d'Elboeuf when they were exhibited in Germany.

Paderni, Camillo (1720–1770) This scholar was in charge of studying and making drawings of the artifacts discovered at Pompeii and Herculaneum.

Piaggio, Antonio (1711–1796) A priest and scholar, he was brought to Naples from the Vatican Library in Rome to decipher the text of the scrolls found at the Villa of the Papyri in Herculaneum.

Tanucci, Bernardo (1698–1793) As the prime minister of Naples, he was left in charge of the excavations when Charles took over the crown of Spain.

Weber, Karl Jacob (1712–1764) A Swiss army engineer recommended by Alcubierre to oversee the excavations at Herculaneum and Pompeii. Weber became interested in the houses and the life in the ancient Roman city. He proposed excavating and mapping whole villas and streets rather than just searching for treasure.

Winckelmann, Johann Joachim (1717–1768) A German scholar who visited Pompeii and wrote about the lack of access to the treasures. After a second visit, he had good words for Weber.

SOURCE NOTES

13 Christopher Charles Parslow.
    *Rediscovering Antiquity: Karl
    Weber and the Excavation of
    Herculaneum, Pompeii, and Stabiae.*
    (New York: Cambridge University
    Press, 1998), 216.

17 Ibid., 34–35.

19 Ibid., 33.

20 Ibid., 35.

20 Ibid.

30 Ibid., 91.

33 Ibid., 103.

34 Ibid., 104.

35 Ibid., 90.

36 Ibid., 69.

43 Ibid., 128.

44 Ibid., 133.

44 Ibid.

50 Ibid., 197.

50 Ibid., 205.

53 Ibid., 206.

53 Ibid.

53 Ibid.

53 Ibid., 209.

55 Ibid., 210.

55 Ibid.

56 Ibid., 270.

56 Ibid., 218.

56 Ibid., 219.

57 Ibid., 224.

58 Ibid., 3.

59 Ibid., 231.

59 Ibid., 232.

59 Ibid., 242.

SELECTED BIBLIOGRAPHY

Brilliant, Richard. *Pompeii AD 79: The Treasure of Rediscovery.* New York: Clarkson N. Potter, 1979.

Carpiceci, A. C., and L. Pennino. *Pompeii - Herculaneum: Today and 2000 Years Ago.* Salerno, Italy: Matonti Editore, n.d.

Coarelli, Filippo, Emidio de Albentiis, Maria Paola Guidobaldi, Fabrizio Pesando, and Antonio Varone. *Pompeii.* Trans. Patricia A. Cockram. New York: Barnes & Noble, 2006.

Deiss, Joseph Jay. *Herculaneum: Italy's Buried Treasure.* New York: Harper & Row, 1985.

Fagan, Brian M., ed. *The Oxford Companion to Archaeology.* New York: Oxford University Press, 1996.

Nappo, Salvatore. *Pompeii: A Guide to the Ancient City.* Trans. A.B.A., Milan. New York: Barnes & Noble, by arrangement with White Star S.p.A., 1998.

Panetta, Marisa Ranieri, ed. *Pompeii: The History, Life and Art of the Buried City.* Verceli, Italy: White Star Publishers, 2005.

Parslow, Christopher Charles. *Rediscovering Antiquity: Karl Weber and the Excavation of Herculaneum, Pompeii, and Stabiae.* New York: Cambridge University Press, 1998.

Rediscovering Pompeii. Rome: L'Erma di Bretschneider, 1992.

FURTHER READING

BOOKS

Behnke, Alison. *Italy in Pictures*. Minneapolis: Twenty-First Century Books, 2003.

Beller, Susan Provost. *Roman Legions on the March*. Minneapolis: Twenty-First Century Books, 2008.

Connelly, Peter. *Pompeii*. New York: Oxford University Press, 1994.

Deem, James M. *Bodies from the Ash: Life and Death in Ancient Pompeii*. Boston: Houghton Mifflin, 2005.

Markel, Rita J. *Your Travel Guide to Ancient Rome*. Minneapolis: Twenty-First Century Books, 2004.

Mellor, Ronald, and Marni McGee. *The Ancient Roman World*. New York: Oxford University Press, 2004.

Nardo, Don. *A Travel Guide to Ancient Pompeii*. San Diego: Lucent Books, 2004.

Rice, Melanie. *Pompeii: The Day a City Was Buried*. New York: Dorling Kindersley Publishing, 1998.

WEBSITES

Archaeology's Interactive Dig
http://www.archaeology.org/interactive/pompeii
Archaeology magazine is responsible for this site, which explores the excavations of Pompeii in the past and present.

EyeWitness to History.com. "The Destruction of Pompeii"
http://www.eyewitnesstohistory.com/pompeii.htm
Read about eyewitness accounts of Pliny the Younger as he experiences the eruption of Mount Vesuvius and the destruction it caused.

Pompeii

http://www.civilization.ca/cmc/pompeii/pompei1e.html

This website, created by the Canadian Museum of Civilization, offers images and information from a traveling exhibition developed by the Soprintendenza Archeologica di Pompei.

Pompeii: Stories from an Eruption

http://www.fieldmuseum.org/pompeii/

See the art, history, lives, and deaths of Pompeii's inhabitants. Use interactive maps and timelines to see the devastation of the volcanic activity to each town.

Soprintendenza Archeologica di Pompei

http://www2.pompeiisites.org/database/pompei/pompei2.nsf

The official site of the Soprintendenza Archeologica di Pompei (available in English) features virtual tours of Pompeii and Herculaneum today, as well as many pictures of objects from the museum's collection.

INDEX

ABOUT THE AUTHOR

Liz Sonneborn is a full-time writer living in Brooklyn, New York. A graduate of Swarthmore College, she has written more than sixty books for both children and adults on a wide variety of subjects. Her books include *The American West*, *A to Z of American Indian Women*, *The Ancient Kushites*, *The Vietnamese Americans*, *Chronology of American Indian History*, *Guglielmo Marconi*, and *The New York Public Library's Amazing Native American History*, which won a 2000 Parents' Choice Award. Sonneborn has also written *The Navajos*, *The Choctaws*, *The Creek*, *The Chumash*, and *The Shoshones*.

PHOTO ACKNOWLEDGMENTS